GW01081185

SKIMMING THE SOUL

Skimming the Soul

TARIQ LATIF

Littlewood
1991

For my Mother and Father

Published by Littlewood Arc, The Nanholme Centre,
Shaw Wood Road, Todmorden, Lancashire OL14 6DA
Design & Print by Arc & Throstle Press Ltd, Todmorden
Typeset by Anne Lister Typesetting, Halifax

Acknowledgements are due to: *The Rialto, Poetry Nottingham, Envoi, Iron, Pennine Platform, The Echo Room, The Wide Skirt, Affirming Flame Anthology, Ambit, Poetry Review and Iota.* Some of the poems have also been broadcast on the BBC Network programme *Write Now.*

CONTENTS

INNOCENCE PEPPERED

My grandfather white bearded
stares, stares deep at thin air.

I am in the field of watermelons.
Great green bulks neat in rows.

The sting of dust is
my urgency of the picking.

I wrench the weighty melon from
its prickly cord and earth's juices.

My grandfather, white turbaned, is
draped in a white cotton chemise.

He surges from realms of the spiritual
to the skeleton of the physical

and with one blow of his right hand
the watermelon cracks open, red,

cool succulent red, grained with
grinning seeds. These he picks.

Red surfaces he smears with spice.
My mouth sweet water quenched is

acid-lined.

KITES

All of India is this day
Out flying kites. Government
Ministers, factory workers
Cha-wallahs, we have all

Traded the value of our lives
For kites. Hexagonal, butterfly
Plain romboid shaped kites.
So many colours cluttering the sky.

A furious battle field
Kites crash into kites
Gashing their paper skins
Breaking their brittle sticks.

It is a skill to manoeuvre
A kite free from trouble or
To guide it with precision
To kill. Stalking the prey

Suddenly circling the victim's string
Looping round and round in tighter
Circles, and now tugging
Your string, back and forth

Like a saw. You can taste blood
When the snared kite drops
In mid-flight, falling in a slow
Majestic descent – losers and winners.

It is easy to forget that we
Are celebrating an arrival and
Departure of seasons: sunshine
Breaking winter's frost. We are

Too much caught up with the petty
Squabbles of our lives. We think
Only of slitting kites – the strings
Telegraph our angry and excited cries.

WATER SNAKES

In this mud dank room
In the mixed smell of straw and oil
The huge wheels of the tube-well
Spin, belts turn
Pipes suck water
From the black ocean underground.

Outside, in the huge trough
The tube-well's mouth bursts
With bright waterfalls
Thunderous water
Crashes onto walls
Drowning air that surges about sea foam.

I can see

Water-snakes
Cascading into the trough.
They guzzle the air
Spit out rainbow sprays

I leap

Into the trough
Water crashes about my
Porous body of clay.
My head overflows with
White pearls, lapidated
By the watery fangs
Of the water-snakes

I could almost
Slush away
Down muddy waterways
Enter the paddy fields, where

The water-snakes ripple
Along green stalks – leap out
To invisibility, leave behind white seeds.

My body water dissolves this rice.
An invisible cord snakes
Out of my navel.
It feeds me soft tissues of manna.

LAHORE 1947

We are farmers.
We live a simple life
Working on the land, in the sun.

We sleep on our straw beds.
Our houses smell, and are
Made of mud and straw.

We don't understand politics.
Politics is something discussed
Between clever people.

They say
There will be a state
For the muslims, up North.

I think it's just talk.
Politicians change their minds
Like a chameleon changes colour.

They will have us move out
Only to move back again.
We have to leave today.

Mother insists I bring
The sewing machine with us.
'It's expensive

I don't want it stolen
While we're away.'
I strap the Singer machine

Awkwardly onto my bicycle.
The house is locked
Full of our possessions

Loaded with the memories
Of births, marriages and deaths.
We form a family convoy.

So much of us, grained
In the walls of our village,
Is lost to the sun.

* * * *

Just outside Lahore
We enter a small village.
It is empty. It looks

A lot like our village.
We break into one house
And are surprised

To find it fully furnished.
My grandfather, bewildered, settles
In an armchair.

My uncles rest on a bed.
My mother examines the utensils.
The table is set for a meal.

A poster of Shiva
Rustles, as if desecrated.
And then we notice

In the corner of the house
A space that looks familiar.
I carefully place

The sewing machine there.
Our hopes to return fade like dusk.
This will have to be home.

IGLOOS AND HAMMOCKS

I can walk the entire length
Of our village across the flat
Roofs of our homes. Each house,
Each wall is made of straw flecked mud.

The dankness of our rooms fills
Our clothes and minds, releases
About us the presence of grand and
Great grandparents. Everyone is related

In our village. The Tonga-Wallah
Has, this day, bought for me a book. I
Cannot read but the pictures tell
Stories. Here is a family in a house

Made out of wood. Children play by
An open doorway. Their mother is
Cooking dinner (just like my mother).
A man is sleeping in a hammock

Happy among his family. Outside
There are other homes. Identical.
A village of happy families, somewhere,
On the other side of the world. I have never

Seen the snow or the sea but here
Is a country made entirely of snow
Ice and sea. A white dome shaped house
Looks like a mosque. Here is a family

Dressed in thick layers of fur. The mother
Plays with her children. The father
Is fishing from a circular hole
Cut in the floor of their house!

A white village of igloos, on the very
Top of the world. The huge Earth
Turns, about itself, about these igloos
And around the one far sun. I close my

Eyes, imagine my hard bed slack
As a hammock, swinging, (the scent
Of my mother's cooking bridges distance).
I imagine the sky segmented like an igloo.

MASUNDA

This is no holy land.

These walls of streets
that sprawl and the dank rooms of homes
are made out of straw grained mud
hand smoothed by our grandfathers
blessed holy with their hot breath

but this is no holy land.

There is a thin bone bagged dog
slurping his own faeces.
A fat grimed carcass festers with flies.
There are the open sewers
thick with slime, and
littered with sleeping mosquitos.

The old women drabbed in grubby saris
sit in the cool yard
smoking a cigarette, chatting, cackling
dreaming of a holy land.

Nightfalls and the mud walls dissolve.
A dog yelps at the golden moon.
Some prowling mosquitos stop
to sip my blood.
The old men resting from the toils
in the field, talk and laugh, and share a pipe.
The hooka smoulders a sugar layered
dry cow dung.

This is my holy home.

SUGAR CANES

With straws dug deep in soil
The sugar canes grub for
And suck earth's blood.

All summer I have prayed
To the gods that dream up clouds.
I have watched my sugar canes grow
Slept with them in their thick nectar sleep.

Our ripened sticks are crammed
With fine juices of mud and sunshine.

This is the month of winter.
I carry a heavy serrated knife.

The sugar canes whisper psalms
Of self offering
Thanking the sun, thanking the mud
Filling me with their crystals of farewells.

"We are dead but for a short time."

And I hack hack hack
And I stack stack stack
And it is evening . . .

My mule complains of the load.

In my mud dried yard
I grind the sugar canes
Crushing out the summer
That splashes like sunshine
Into huge clay jars.

My wife simmers the sweet juices.
Hundreds of bubbles surface and burst
Dissolving in the air the nectar of their soul
Making of my house a field of ghost sugar canes.

My wife scoops out
Warm crystals of brown sugar.
She feeds our two sons.
The boys are marrowing
The sun and the mud.

SKIMMING THE SOUL

She slops the curd
Into the churn
Sprinkles a little salt

And with ropes in hands
She pulls, lets go
Pulls to and fro.

Shafts of light sinking in her face
Scour the stains that deny her grace.

Lumps are battered to a whiteness
All exposed and battled to a rightness.

Ropes wind unwind, climb unclimb,
Her spirit swirls out of the slime

Spinning around the shaft, on and on
Flows of pure finesse, all blotches gone

And still she tugs from side to side
Until the churn oozes thick tides.

She then scoops out
The creamy white muckan
Places it gently on a silver dish.

CINDERED – BONES

My mother holds me tight
In her cold arms, and looks
Out to the sky.

A red moon hides behind a flurry of black snow.
The sky is crammed with these
Bat-like bits that have sucked out the sun.

I turn to my grandfather
Even he the military man is silent
And my uncles are children
Witnessing a funeral pyre in the sky

And there, in among the silent wind
Mixed within ash, there are
Soft flesh flakes
Dry broken psalms that
Swell in my mother's head
Her mascara splatters
Onto my face,and my throat tightens
Black images clot my mind

I think of the village which is
Not so far away, gutted
Glowing with cinders
Strewn with cindered-bones

An angry wind is brushing up
Black flakes and painting the air
The air that this afternoon
Had erupted to flames
Had caressed sleeping farmers
To crisps of flesh on bone.

The sky loosens itself from the ash
Black flakes settle on our upturned faces
I tremble catching the drone of an aeroplane.

ELEPHANTS AND HIPPOS

To lie down, alone,
Is to risk
Being eaten alive.

This hippo has no strength
Not even to move.
Dust burns his sun sapped body.
He catches a glimpse
Of lurking hyenas, red fangs . . .

*

How the elephants find
This unmarked land I'll never know
But here they are
Arriving in a whirl of dust
Expecting to see a river
Finding only dust and a handful of hippos.

Madness drifts
Like heat waves
Between the arid elephants.

*

Death stalks
Through the night
White incisors, demonic red eyes . . .

Nothing disturbs the elephants
Huddled together in a common sleep
In a common dream.

*

Dawn brings the desert sun.

The huge elephants begin
To pound the dry river bed.
There is water here
They can smell it.

Mid-day. High sun.
The elephants are lost
In thick dust palls
Losing themselves in their
Pounding, in their faith.

By evening
The ground begins to give mud.
Death lurks
With a thirsty stomach
But nothing disturbs
The elephants as they wade
Together in their dream of water . . .

*

Dawn brings the desert demons:
Bald eagles; vultures; blood smeared
Hyenas; thin lions . . .

The one remaining hippo
Has challenged a lion
For some water.

Nothing disturbs the elephants'
Communion. They must move on
To where I'm not sure
But they disappear, like
Pilgrims, into the sun.

*

The one remaining hippo
Wallows in mud. Waiting. Watching.
Watching the salivating fangs.

ELEPHANT CULLING

Torn fig trees, sucked sapless,
Are scattered on the ground
Drying like broken white bones.

The elephants drowse, in among
their spoils of gutted fig trees.
They do not move in their sleep
This mid-day sleep.

There is the smell of urine
Sweetening in the mid-day sun.
Baking mud on wrinkled skin
flakes to dust
Red mouths open
Gasping out, sucking in hot air.

The dry females are dreaming
Of milk, of milking their young
Of milking this arid land
that there is
              grass, leaves, fig-trees . . .

The hungry males are dreaming
Of a lush, fruit-filled jungle
Where the antelope and the lioness stop
to share with them cool figs.
They dream of water, water enough
to splash away earthy grime.

The white-hatted men
Weave like snakes towards
the sleeping elephants.
The men raise their metal sticks
Breaking the air with whistling needles
And the elephants
Scream like wild trumpets

As if they herald the white angels
As if they cry in joy for the stings

that jolt
them awake
in their dreams.

P A

Long distance call
Pa is dead.
My mother wails across
The vast west east divide.
They cry
Mourning the loss
Down an infinite telephone line.

My father is a mountain of grief.
With my face in sunshine
I have caught rainbows
Between my wet eyelashes.

My father's great towering
Shoulders block the sun.

I tremble
In his silent eruptions.
The hot lava of his pain
Crawls down my cragged throat.

Pa is buried.
There is nothing tangible to let go.

My father sitting in the cold sun
Fingers a lego toy.

It was a long time ago.

THE LIZARD

Was mid-way up a wall.
My father was poised
Air gun in hand.

Pellets broke plaster.
The lizard did not stir.
Was it because of fear

Or defiance? Submission
Or hope? There was a burst
Of hot blood shot through

The wall of my head.
Then there was this hole
From which childhood drained.

FORGETTING

And I remember
the dog tails strung around his waist.
Evidence of his trade. The government man
out to kill stray dogs. Each tail was
worth so many rupees.

We followed him, mesmerised by his
double-barrel gun and his hunter's
instincts. We were children stalking
through his imagined jungle land as he
picked his way through the street.

And then, our neighbour's dog, the
little white dog, ran out to us
and would not stop barking at
the man. The government man who was
poised like a brave hunter.

I remember the thunder of the gun
and the air breaking in my throat,
then silence. I don't remember the
little white dog that must
have slumped there in blood.

MISS WOOD

Primary school was a world
Made up of plasticine and crayons.
Soft warm little towns, where
We would imagine ourselves

As grown-ups living happy lives.
We would draw pictures
Of match stick people, playing
Among rainbows. And Primary school

Was the lovely Miss Wood, tall, black
Hair and her lips always strikingly red.
To us boys she was the undiscovered
Cinderella. But to the girls she was

The wicked step-mother of Snow White.
During playtime, after biscuits and milk,
We used to chase the girls
Pretending to be wolves.

As I remember it, Miss Wood
Used to smack us boys, but
Had only threatened the girls. Once
I saw the intense seriousness

On Miss Wood's face crack
A smile, as she smacked
Philip's legs. It was Sarah
Who had noticed that Philip

Was being made to stay behind
At playtime. Soon after he
Just vanished. Nothing was said.
And we shall

Never forget the way Miss Wood
Left mid-lesson: excusing herself
And disappearing, far out in the
Play field, into the falling snow.

SWANS AND CROWS

I

And the swans
Scuttle across the water, spread
Their bright wings and bloat
The blue air with their hot throated
Laughter. And just beyond the lake
In a field that has become desert
There are scrawny crows heaped
Onto themselves. Their pained
Sighing disturbs only the dry air
Which resettles around them like dust.

II

There are giants playing football
In the fields below. They stride
Across many fields, in an instant,
Kicking a huge ball of wheat. I
Watch them from a mountain top.
An African, crawling on hands and knees,
Approaches me. The top half of his back
And head are missing, so that to my
Horror I can see inside his rib cage.
I reach inside, clutch his heart,
Wanting to exercise euthanasia
Wanting myself to wake up and to think
Of this as just a bad dream.

A DREAM DURING RAMAZAN

Eating bananas and mincemeat
I walk through a field close
To my Primary School.
From the dish I carry
I scoop another handful
but find instead of food
Excrement and fat white worms.
The scene changes
To a dark street.
Car keys in hand I freeze
Instead of my car there is
A huge space. A woman
Screams and hobbles
Across the road. Her left
Foot is smashed – bone splinters
Have pierced bone. She continues
To shriek and limp and jolt
Across the road between fast cars.
"Don't move" I yell but she leaps
Into the arms of an ambulance man.
He spreads his divine hand
Over her anguished face
And brings comfortable sleep.
The loud sirens wake me up.
My human clock checks with the digital
Two fifteen in the morning.
It is time to eat a little
Then start my fast from sunrise
To sunset, when I shall open the fast
With banana slices and meat.

A WAKING DREAM

Tiny pale stars begin to fade
In a huge luminous sky.
My bed is a raft

Made out of bones. My hands
And feet are tied. I am
Drifting toward a white beach.

Sea waves foam white wreaths.
A shrieking gull lunges at me
I jolt up – my arms flapping the bed sheets.

CORNFIELD

A cloud packed sky.
Rain, warm summer rain,
Drips across the faces

Of the firm cornpods. Sleepy
Heads between green leaves
Are full of empty yellow dreams.

Rain sprinkles a galaxy
Of stars on the dry ground.
Warm earth scents climb up

Into the thick blanket of corn smells.
Nothing disturbs this sleeping crowd
Not even this man who, fleeing

For his life, ploughs through the
Cornfield. Some white robed men,
Swinging long knives, follow close

Behind. The man falls, sprawls over
In an awkward crucifix. Knives
Rain down, splitting him like

Watermelons. Red stars spurt
On white robes. Life gives up
Between cut cobs and broken bones.

There is lightning. Air thunders
Around the men, who pause, knives
Hung in mid-air, in mid-swing,

Above their white pointed hats
But then nothing can fill
Their hollow heads (walled with hate).

And so the knives come down.
The cornfield sleeps on. It rains
Briefly. The sun drowns in blood.

RAIN IN A CORNFIELD

Warm rain has made water of her skin.
His fingers dip and glide, caressing
And cupping her fluidness. Deep within
This cornfield no-one will see them undressing.

An artist, meditating in the cornfield,
Is filled with the scents of wet soil and
Green corn-pods. Warm rain has revealed
A yellow oil painting that runs between his hands.

A man, fleeing for his life,
Has leapt into this cornfield. A white
Robed man follows, swinging a long knife.
From severed flesh gushes amniotic light.

A NEW PERSPECTIVE

A mouse in a wheat-field
Flees from a combine.

Liquid black eyes burst
Like sunshine between clouds.
(I will never see you again.)

The tail, the limbs, all made
Mincemeat-sprawled; like
My emotions; in a tight
Puckered cube.

This cube view
Offers a new perspective.
An element of distrust
Between a lover, between people . . .

As I sift through
The memories of you and me
I recall your last kiss
Cold as steel.

RASPBERRIES

The garden pond, black
Velvets moonlight.

I cup my hands in prayer
Scoop out water from the pond.

The moon, a ghostly coin
For Charon, trembles between my hands.

Water tumbles to my stomach
Crystallizes a pool of memory.

I crawl on hands and knees
Drawn by the cold nectar of the raspberries.

Those fat leeches
Pulse with the warmth of you.

I mouthe, burst you with my tongue
Let your sweet acids gush

From throat to blood to the stupid
Wound of my Cupid struck heart.

The purple lips of the sky
Suck at my purpling heart

And from the slow burn of white
There is a spread of blue.

The garden pond, jade
Velvets sunlight.

I cup my hands in prayer

MY CHOICE AT 13+

Sat out in the midday sun
We felt European.
The sun had scorched
Dry the wells in Greece,
Had burnt fires in France,

In Devon.
And the summer of '76 was
Green – the grass,
The willow trees,
The school dinner salads.

And then we felt international
Lindon, Simon, Amrish and I.
Between us there were
Caribbean beaches, Jerusalem,
And the hot Indian bazaars.

The summer of '76 was
When we chose the course of our
Lives, well more or less!
Was it to be French or Biology "O" level?
A degree in Medicine or Law?

A European breeze ruffled
Through our white shirts, our decisions . . .
I left our group and walked
Towards the willow tree

Where the breeze, rushing
Out of my shirt,
Whispered among the willow leaves –
My heart's desire
Lovely Claire lying in the shade.

Cool, slender
Her arms were folded across her chest
Her soft face turned towards mine–
"What you looking at Paki?"
"Hmm-nothing, nothing really".

EXAM PHOBIA

Working late into the night
I used to nod off in the laps
Of open books. I would breathe
In endless formulas and integers.

And my black and white dreams
Were made of these: a crowd
Of numbers, fully clothed, going
About their business along a busy

High street. As I ambled past
The Gamma Police Station I noticed
A poster: Criminal wanted for evasion
Of study. The dot matrix picture

Was of me. "Stop skiver!" someone
Shouted – then from nowhere alphas and
Thetas dressed as bobbies were running
Toward me – I leapt over a pi symbol

Dodged some neutron bullets and
Darted down an alley – dead end.
There was no escape. I was walled
In by huge fat Thetas.

One of them produced a large differential
Equation, another produced Newton's balls
We have ways of making you work."
"No no no I won't work." Immediately

Buckets of integers were emptied
On me, followed by rapid questions:
"What is the uncertainty principle?"
"Explain the reciprocal lattice."

"Why does light bend around stars?"
My head shrank and expanded as I
Fell into the infinities of space
Through the sub-atomic and the inter-stellar.

I used to wake up reciting formulas
Then I'd rush to my book shelves
Rummage for those bloody notes and to my
Relief I would remember having graduated.

A REQUIEM FOR NANA

We are dressed in black
On this bright summer's day.
There is laughter in the leaves

Outside our bay window.
A river of sunshine flows through
Our front room, and

Waterfalls onto the back wall.
The shadows of leaves
Look like salmon

Leaping between splashes
Of light. A lush valley
Unfolds itself before us.

Dave moves between mossed rocks
Coffee cup in hand.
James is sitting on a stone slab

Near the record player.
The music we are listening to
Is Rodrigo's guitar concerto.

Betty leans against rock
Her hand held out, boney
In a bar of light, fumbles

To touch the faint silhouette
Of her mother, as the ghost lines fade
Among the shadows of dust.

A red rose
Threads her eyes
Water-petals break.

MUSIC FOR A WOMAN

A stream descends
A scale of rocks.
Water flutes open

Like skirts, folding
Over stones, tearing
Into ribbons that glitter.

A milkyness pours
Over like gathered
White harp strings

Waterfalls into a deep
Emerald pool. Water: moves
With the slow grace of swans;

Darkens, losing colour
Under the bridge; enters
A dusk full of ghosts.

The surface whispers with
Violins orchestrated around
Scarlet stones. Here water

Ropes into caves. Moon
Splinters glint like shark's
Teeth. Voices gargle in

Among the sagging leaves.
Light is lost. I
Begin to lose my words . . .

A WOMAN SINGS ON SESAME STREET

With eyes closed she undresses her dream
In a song. Words fill the air
With the freshness of morning dew
Strewn across the prairie.

She sings about a village, unfenced,
Unbordered, full of people exchanging
Cultures with their hand-shakes and
Hellos. And the children offer fruit

To the mice, Eagle and Bear
And this is the kingdom where
Her prince lives. Her mind
Begins to strain, she loses

Her words, begins to hum
Sways back and forth between dream
Land and studio set. She opens her
Eyes and is embarrassed by her nakedness.

She puts away her guitar, puts away
Her dream. Picks up a book, reads
Aloud, ABC, A is for apple. She teaches
The children the alphabet of our sins.

PAUL

A drum solo out of time.
He strikes the snare drum
Again and again, thumping at
His hollow life, thrashing the tom-toms

In spasms, like the mad heart thumps
Of a cardiac. Cymbals crash.
A splash of red light
Flashes across the stage.

The hall fills with the hollow
Sounds of an empty drum kit.
A club band, a pub band
A finale, this adieu.

Silence leaps out in mid-note.
Paul's arms spread like a crucifix.
He puts down the drum sticks
Limps to the front of the stage.

Lights fade like dusk.
A spot light traces the moon-craters
Of his face, that hangs
Just above the microphone.

"In the light, is my favourite song
And as you know I can't sing
So let's have plenty of reverb
From the sound controls please."

And so Paul sings
This song about a person,
Trapped behind walls, searching
For keys among severed wings.

His last note lingers
Like the echoes of a scream.
Red light fills his face
Making his beard look like embers

A red glow spreads across stage
Crawls in the tinder bound crowd.
Paul's wife Jane fumbles with
A cigarette and a dry flint.

An old couple by a crowded door
Struggle with their volatile emotions.
Paul sits behind his drum kit
Drum sticks held like dynamite

JANE

When we stepped
Into your kitchen
We were, drenched
By dinner steams,

Overwhelmed by the warm
Mix of delicious scents:
Green spice of peppers;
Fried meat and boiling potatoes.

Quickly you ushered us
Into the lounge, insisting
On keeping the meal a surprise.
We waited like two hungry children.

I sat in an armchair
Full of sunshine. My eyes
Wandered among the complex as
Of your cluttered table.

Letters waiting to be answered,
A sewing machine among
Emerald buttons and cloth
And mountains of books.

A copy of Owen's Poetry leant
Against Delia Smith's cookery
Book. Both leant against a vase
Full of withered white flowers.

When you entered the room
With plates full of stew, the air
Was saturated with the essence
Of you. Soft, warm, wet around

My lips, meats in a sauce
Only you could make. I watched
You, greedily swallowed you
In generous mouthfuls of kisses.

SHEILA

Dust cloth and hoover
In hand, there is
Always something to do
In the house, in the kitchen.

She sees her family
In ones and twos, and only
At the kitchen table
As they appear and disappear,

Like hotel guests, leaving only
Dirty plates and clothes. Life is
Measured in cups of soap powder.
She is stranded in a sea of hung laundry.

A lighthouse keeper, she
Picks up the phone and talks
To imaginary friends, and they
Understand believe her when

She says, there is a ghost
In the house. How, sometimes,
She would find the beds set,
Some of the washing done.

But Sheila doesn't understand
Why, when she stands on the top
Of the stairs, she wants to scream.
She will tell her son

Before he leaves to do his exams.
Entering his room, she finds him
Head down, like an ostrich, buried
In books of Advanced Calculus.

Bit by bit she turns light
From her lighthouse onto him.
A storm crashes through
His rigid mathematical framework.

He tries to differentiate
Tries to integrate, but
Nothing computes, and besides
He really must be going.

Later in the afternoon
Sheila is mesmerized
By onions as they burn and spit
Like the broken bits of her mind.

RACHEL
to Ian and Karen

Damp warm air
Breezed through our
Patio door, riffled

Among the papers and books
On the table, silenced
Our wide-eyed baby

Filled the room
With the imminence
Of rain. It was

A sudden downpour
Thunder and summer rain
Which finished abruptly.

We stepped into the garden
Just as, droplets
Were dripping from

The holly leaves
And warm soil
Smells were mixing

With the sharpened
Scents of the roses
And skylarks were

Leaping into a crystal
Rinsed sky. White
Clouds were breaking up

And the wind, brushing
Among them, surged
Downwards, past

The vibrant wings
Of the skylarks,
And boomed all around

Our garden, washing
Us with a clear blue
Coolness. Just then

As the washing line
Was swinging, sunshine
Was spreading delicious

Colours among the wet
Crimson and white roses.
We felt the faint textures

Of aromas moving around
Us, and as the well
Of our hearts filled up

With nectars, Rachel
Opened her tiny hand
Silhouette against the sky

Reaching for the sun
Her delicate fingers
Spread out like petals.

CAMPSITE AT PRAA SANDS

Dusk. Pale moonlight.
I was lost in a storm
Of self-pity. My adolescence
A ship battered by powerful
Waves of emotions. The car

Turned up the embankment
Slow as a hearse. Inside
Were my friends, dark,mysterious
Still as rocks among troubled water.
"Where are you going?"

"I'm going to the shore
To look at the moon."
Silence between me and them.
Silence between our minds.
Their thoughts shaped eyes

And could only stare
At me ship-wrecked
Among jagged rocks. And so
We went opposite ways. I to the
Shore, and they to the tent.

But I had wanted to say more
I wanted to say that I
Am going to the shore, to look at
The frightful moon, to look at that
Skull hung on a black noose

I am going to the shore
To stand before the dark sea
To stare at the moonlight
Draped like linen over the black
Waves. This terrible silence

Between us, makes me feel like
Dust falling in space
Between Earth and Moon
Between stars. In the beginning
There was the word, and the word was

loneliness.

TOTAL ECLIPSE OF THE MOON

Shadows. Slow
Movement of shadows.

I cannot perceive
The immensity of space
Between Earth and Moon
Between us and the sun.

Shadows: penumbra
And umbra. The moon
Is moving into shadows.

I try to imagine,
Looking out to the moon
From Manchester, the long
Shadow of the Earth
In space, the sun
Behind me shining
Over Australia
And the moon moving
And the Earth turning.

Sinister shadows are creeping
Across the moon, like an army
Of black killer ants, letting
Blood around the borders, reducing
The moon to a brittle crescent.

Suddenly my mother
Collapses in a heap of pain.
My touch is cold
To her hand. She sheds
Tears pale as moonlight.

Something, beyond me,
Is happening to my mother
Something like a dried
Black moon, breaking up
Like blackened bones. I am
Lost in the infinities of space.

Outside the moon
Moves out of the
Darkest shadow

But the shadow
Thrown into our house
Remains, like a terrible
Black shroud of death.

NOVEMBER

Is the stark nudity
Of the trees, along our street.

It is the winter air
Crystallising a fine frost

In my throat. It is
Arriving home early

Finding you all packed
And ready to go. Our eyes

Not meeting. Our awkward
Shoulders knocking against

The narrow hall.
Our faces, tight as fireworks,

Moving opposite ways.
November is a door shutting.

It is a house full of absences.
It is a long bleak night

And a stale pool of home brew.
November is a fist in my throat.

It is a smoke clogged sky
Filled with S.O.S. flares.

AN ASYLUM MADE OF FOG

Everything outside is the same
Identical and white.

To step out of my room
Is to risk losing myself
In a maze of white walls.

This is a nice room – really
It's just this other man
Starch faced and always
Dressed in white.
He never speaks
Just bares his jagged teeth
And whenever the men visit
He just disappears.

Here they come again
In their white overalls
And their comfortable smells
Of chloroform.
They stalk around me
Like white ravens, picking
At my words, at my bones

"There's something we want you to do
Something we want
We want to help . . . "

I make thick fog
So thick
I lose everyone
And myself

I am a mouse
In an infinite maze

I sense the spread of wings
I run, always in the growing
Pale shadow of wings
Always running . . .

SNOW

I

When it snows here, in Manchester,
it snows the same as in the films
on my black and white T.V.

I am watching a fairy story
from Europe. A voice translates.
The Prince, in the snow, stumbles across a dead girl.

I

At the kitchen table
my mother and father converse in Punjabi.
I translate to an imaginary audience.

Outside it begins to snow.
My parents stop talking about in-laws,
hold hands like two characters in a story.

A GREY MAN

Suddenly he was there
Sheepish by the doorway
Grey suit, white hair.

He really had nothing to say.
He smiled, we shook hands
And went our separate ways.

He disappeared into his grey land
Delicate as ashes, common as sand.

AVON PLEATING

They pleat skirts
And he would while at work
Wear a skirt
Over his trousers with today's
Neat little pleat.

Just another 200 to pleat
His fingers gather cloth
Fold over fold
He presses with a hot iron
Steam puffs into his face

And he becomes machine
Skirt after skirt after skirt

Steam rushes into the pleats
Of his face – he feels no hurt

Again steam fingers grope
At a desperate pace, searching for

A little hope, bits of a dream
But they clench only the air

In themselves, drench only
The cavities of his bleached head.

Automated he thinks of nothing
Leaves the factory floor

With a head full of steam.
Home and then to the pub

Home and then to bed.
He returns the next day

The same, into his life of steam
Day in day out, day in decade out.

PROFIT AND LOSS

There is something here
He does not understand.
Part of the answer is stacked
Among the rows of shelves

Among the thousands of zips, cotton reels
Buttons in their multitude of shapes
Colours. It is the way
They are meticulously arranged

Clearly labelled,made profitable
By her hand,her good business sense.
How could she, then, give up
Family, business, and friends

For the price of one man?
It just does not compute.
He takes two reels, paces up
And down along his huge warehouse.

The scent of thread weaves
In his mind, exact, the pattern
Of her smile, her face
His precious little girl.

He lunges at a bag of buttons
Red buttons pour like blood
Bouncing off his face, gathering at
His knees. He picks them up. One by one

Drop by drop, he utters her name . . .

UNCLE MUSTKA

Hides behind a brick wall
To surprise his son.
The wall is scrawled with
'PAKIS OUT CURRY HOUSE NF'

But this does not bother
Uncle Mustka. He has just
Returned from Lahore, Pakistan,
And he waits with delight for

His son to answer the door.
Sunlight surprises Uncle Mustka
He moves away from the wall
Stands in the sun

The warmth fills his eyes
Mouth, bones and he dreams
Of a warm blue sky spread
Over Manchester, over Lahore,

Of sunshine, that bridges East and West
Kisses his brow, his paddy fields.
In the tight of his eyes
Uncle Mustka stalks the wet

Recalls the stoop of his grandfather
Rice white as bones . . .
"Dad what are you doing here
You're not due back for another week?"

THE OUTSIDERS

I

Here they come in their
Long salwalers, beards
And obligatory hats.

Straight out of the streets
Of Lahore, only in Manchester,
Conversing in Punjabi

Exchanging jokes and doing
Their best to make Wilmslow Road
A bazaar just like home.

II

When you step into some sweat-shops
It's like walking into a factory
That may as well be in Pakistan.

There are Pakistani workers, Pakistani music
And that carefree Pakistani attitude:
"What cheque?" It's difficult

To keep a straight face when
The director of the company is craned
Over a sink washing his feet

And conducting a business meeting!
"What cheque?" he inquired with false
Anxiety. I have to grit my teeth

To stop myself from laughing.
God and business don't mix, not when
It came to cheques anyway

And as it was prayer time, there
Was no chance. So I said Salam
Went home and prayed to God for a cheque.

III
I hate going to pubs.
I hate being the only
Coloured person in a packed pub.

I've learnt to ignore
The funny looks I get, but when
A gang of lads start singing

Songs like "Paki's on the orange
Juice, Pakis out" followed by
The national Anthem – I leave.

IV
And when she threw up
Her hands and exclaimed
"I'm English I know the law"

It was the last straw.
My mother went for her
And I struggled to restrain

My mum. When the shouting was over
When I'd shut the door on the
Quiet middle class avenue

I went upstairs to my
Bedroom and closed my
Arms around my head.

V

Shall I eat with knife and fork
Or with my hands?
Shall I trade the kingdom of Heaven
For a slice of ham?
Shall I leap into the voluminous night
Between East and West?
Will I find refuge after my flight?
If I take the chance
And sever my roots
            will they grow
In the warmth of your white arms?
Does the fear in my face show?

What do I do now that I
Am hung upside down over grey
Muddled space? My feet are roped
Into family blood. My arms have
Grown wings and I just hang, limp,
Swaying between two worlds.

ALLEY

It was only last night when
A black man was chased down
Our alley by a mob of white youths.
And when they were gone, only moments

Later two men scouted the yards
Of our homes, then chose not to rob us.
How strange the alley looks in the sultry
Afternoon. I am surprised at the nakedness

Of our lives. Mrs McGee sits in her
Yard peeling potatoes, and Mrs Lee is
Frying some beans. Downstairs my
Mother peppers the air with ginger

And garlic. It mixes well with
Our neighbour's coconut spice
And the sun stirs into my reddening
Skin the warm mix of our continents.

LETTING GO

She gasps
Quick short gasps.
He senses her struggle
But can only witness
The air
            that burns in his lungs
The air
            that fills this room
                shrink
About her pouted lips.

Her pulse loses itself in a maze of wires.
The green screen registers a flat line.
Soon he will have to disconnect his daughter.

He hangs his face
Close to her tiny lips
Sucks at her breath, whispers
"Come with me."
And the ghost of her mixes
With the pulse of his, and they
Move to the window.

"This is the green of England
I am a stranger here,
Do you see the blue sky?

It spreads far
And is hot over my land.
I am sorry I cannot take you there
Your granna ma, granna pa, and all
Your cousins are thinking of you.

We are farmers. I wanted
To show you a field of maize,
Of sugarcanes, watermelons . . .
Put to your lips the goodness
Of our land, perhaps your bones
Might have grown . . ."

He pauses, warm birth fluids
Wet his eyes, he feels
The gentle tug of coil
Between his sweaty palms.
The cord breaks so easily.

WEEDS

So many, thronged in my throat.
I wouldn't mind
If it wasn't for the pain.

How they thrive
Feeding on my sentiment.
I hack at them with logic.

But they spring up
Overnight, always clogging
My throat. It is

As I feared. I will
Have to burn away
This sentiment, till up the roots.

If only it were as easy as
Drinking gasolene and throwing
Down a match.

TARIQ LATIF was born in a small village just outside Lahore, Pakistan, in 1962. He spent his childhood on his grandfather's farm. In 1970 the family moved to Manchester. Tariq gained a Physics Degree from Sheffield University in 1984. He has worked in a Cash and Carry, Fashion Shops, and as a part-time roadie. At present he is self-employed running a labelling business. He started writing poetry three years ago.